# SPIRITUAL ABUSE
## in the
# CHURCH

*Dr. Angela R. Williams*

Kingdom Builders Publications LLC

Spiritual Abuse in the Church
Copyright © 2017 by Angela R. Williams
Kingdom Builders Publications

Paperback ISBN –978-0-692-82546-4
E-Book ISBN – 987-0-692-82547-1
Library of Congress Control Number – 2017930854

**Resources**
The Living Bible and the New King James Version are used by permission

**Cover Designer**
LoMar Designs

**Photographer**
Portrait Innovations™

Printed in USA

For conferences, workshops, seminars, and ministry bookings, contact Dr. Angela Williams:
Email: angwilliams52@yaho.com
Facebook.com/authorangiewilliams
Instagram: Pastor Angela Williams@angwilliams2
Twitter.com/angelawilliams@angwilliams52
Linkedin.com/dr.angelawilliams
youTube.com/spiritualabuseinthechurchwithpastorangela

Websites:
www.kingdombuilderspublications.com

# This Book Belongs to:

Thank you for your support.

## DEDICATION

This book is dedicated to my church families:
St. Paul Baptist Church - The church I grew up in from a child which provided wisdom and knowledge into the way Christians should live and conduct themselves. I learned how to love people and treat them the way I wanted to be treated. I also learned that I had to have a relationship with God for myself. St. Paul taught me many spiritual lessons.

Other Churches – some of the few churches God sent me to for a season of training and discovery into the insights I never knew about. They were some of the places I received training and instruction as Moses did on the backside of the desert. They afforded me many eye-opening experiences that would change the very nature of my destiny and future assignments.

Rejoice Christian Center - the church the Lord spoke to me about years ago in dreams and visions. It is the place where the Word is taught and lives are changed. This church has the opportunity to prepare men and women to serve the Lord in its fullest capacity and share the Word with love and compassion. I praise God for all of its members and the other churches that will be infused into its life and ministry.

# Table of Contents

# ACKNOWLEDGMENTS

*I* acknowledge that God alone gets the glory for the many lives that will be delivered and set free as well as the multitude of people that will return back to the church, give and receive forgiveness, foster a closer relationship with the Lord, and revive the church and its spirituality.

The Lord has opened an avenue that will usher in the restoration of family, friends, and loved ones back into the kingdom of God. Because of who God is, the church now has the opportunity to make the corrections necessary to return the body of Christ back to normal Christian living, where everybody is somebody and Jesus is Lord.

Thank you Lord for the ability to share the thoughts and ideas you've placed inside me with the world so that we can all become whom you created us to be freely without intimidation, manipulation, humiliation, and domination. This book is written to 1) expose Satan and his tactics and to 2) heal the hurting.

# FOREWORD

T his is a distinct honor and sheer delight for me to speak on behalf of my friend, Angela Williams. Before discussing my favorite chapter of her imperative work, Spiritual Abuse in the Church, first, Angela R. Davis is a woman of great passion and creativity. You only need to be in her company for moments and that infectious joy will overshadow you, and you will be hooked to remain her audience. She is graceful and an entertaining speaker; maybe that's why she is an educator and preacher. Her zestful and tenacious lifestyle is a formula one would subscribe to for success in one's own life.

Secondly, Angela is a prolific and transparent writer. Her first work, Freed, Not Locked Up Anymore is a book for all times. This book of life experiences dropped in lyrical rhyme made it easier for us to peek or tip-toe in her past and journey with her to the other side of through. I greatly applaud the success of this collection of poetry. If I could recommend any up and coming author, it would be this award-winning writer, Angela Williams.

The authority of Spiritual Abuse in the Church is a sad commentary of the heart problem of man and his inability to really know humanity or God. Author Williams gives an inside scoop of the language and act of a dysfunctional culture trying to look God-normal. It is honest, shocking, and thought provoking. Please be advised, you will be found as a character on any page of this book. Deciding how change should happen is yours to render, but the truth remains; victim, victor, innocent, guilty, the needy and the greedy are found in the clutches of this book.

The dichotomy of this noble work is like a well-aged wine or a sweet and salty nut. Sip and savor. Chew and envelop yourself in the tastefulness of Angela's style of pain, but for sure answers to a heart problem called Abuse.

Chapter 10 RECOGNIZING A HEALTHY CHURCH is one of my favorite chapters because it gives the reader hope and help on resources in what the ugly looks like and how to spot what healthy fellowship is and is not. So ladies and gentlemen, boys and girls, dive in!

Angela, thank you for the release of this global message. Even though everyone will not subscribe to its knowledge, questions, and answers, those that will, can be freed from their bondage, and God will have His glory. Won't it be exciting to partake in that honor He will bestow upon this God-breathed work?

**Louise M Smith,**
*Award Winning Author, Minister, and lyricist*
*Founder of Pen of a Ready Writer Society*

## INTRODUCTION

Spiritual Abuse takes place daily at somebody's church or in someone's congregation. I never knew what it was until I got older and really started paying attention to my surroundings. I have heard slurred comments, devastating remarks, put downs, offensive words, and threats coming from church leaders aimed at congregation members. These were the people we were supposed to look up to for godly advice, directions, and the Word of God weekly. Quickly I became afraid to share what was on my mind with anyone, for fear they would tell what I said and make me the next person to be intimidated, manipulated, or abused by leaders. I grew up in a community where only those with an education, some money, a top paying job, or status in the church and community was acknowledged as somebody. Anyone else was a nobody. I was reared in the projects, so that made me unfit for the high polluting, upper class list as a member of the church. How I dressed, where I lived, who my friends were and what family I was born in seemed to be the criteria for being recognized in the church or playing a vital role as a leader. I was told I couldn't sing, yet I lead songs and share solos today. I was told I would never be anything or go anywhere in life, but today I am an educator, preacher, singer, writer, speaker, and great cook among other talents still being released. When I completed my first book, God placed on my heart the ability to share with others what spiritual abuse is and how to be delivered from it. It is not an easy thing to admit, even to one's self, that you've been spiritually abused, but the freedom and deliverance from it compares to nothing else. Spiritual Abuse knows no color, creed, religion, or race. It is ever present in the churches all over the world. Black, White, Hispanics, Jewish, or any other race of people that have attended church have been exposed to some type of spiritual abuse over the years.

I'm not upset about church as a place to come together and worship God, but I do wonder why spiritual abuse has to take place in the house of God and no one stops it. We love to sing, shout, and dance, but we lie when it comes to owning up to the truth about spiritual abuse. Too    many people have been wounded in the house of God and nothing has been done about it. A change has to take place. More people are leaving churches and never returning, leaving the ministry, leaving valuable teaching and training for foolishness and idiotic hype. God did not plan it this way. Why are we falling for the tricks of Satan? He only has hell to offer.

No church is perfect, but spiritual abuse does not have to be one of its downfalls. It's time we make a clean break away from our sinful nature.

## SPIRITUAL ABUSE RECOVERY

A realistic approach to **change** using Scriptures that will release any kind of spiritual abuses from one's life and allow you to return to your rightful place, the Lord Jesus Christ, and help you get involved with a new church, understanding that every church is not like the one you left. **This book will expose Satan and his tactics upon the churches and lead you to a place of receiving healing for yourself, forgiving others, and loving God again, this time without abuse...**

LET GO OF THE ABUSE AND WRAP YOURSELF IN CHRIST

## WHAT IS SPIRITUAL ABUSE?
### Chapter One

<hr>

Definition:

*S*piritual abuse occurs when a person in religious authority or a person with a unique spiritual practice misleads and maltreats another person in the name of God or Church or in the mystery of any spiritual concept. Spiritual abuse often refers to an abuser using spiritual or religious rank in taking advantage of the victim's spirituality (mentality and passion on spiritual matters) by putting the victim in a state of unquestioning obedience to an abusive authority.

Spiritual abuse includes:

**Psychological abuse and emotional abuse** with the purpose of unnatural domination and control of the victim for self-gratification by a leader

**Physical abuse** that includes physical injury using bodily harm

**Sexual abuse** any act by deeds or words that demean, humiliate or shame the natural worth and dignity of a person as a human being through sexual involvement

**Submission to spiritual authority** without any right to disagree; intimidation;

**Unreasonable control** of a person's basic right (personal autonomy) to make their own decisions (freewill) on spiritual or natural matters;

**False accusation and repeated criticism** by negatively labeling a person as disobedient, rebellious, lacking faith, demonized, apostate, enemy of the church or a deity (a god);

**Isolationism, separation, disenfranchisement, or estrangement** from family and friends outside the group due to cult-religious or spiritual affiliation and native beliefs;

**Exclusivity and elitism**: dismissal of outsiders'

criticism on the basis that the assessment, opinions, and criticism of the critic is invalid

**Esotericism**: withholding information and giving of information only to a selected few; hidden agendas and requirements revealed to members only through doctrines, beliefs, and/or practices;

**Practices** of spiritualism, mysticism, and/or unproven or unorthodox methods.

**Exaltation** of the primary leader(s) to a God-like status in the group and over the group.

**Financial exploitation and enslavement** of supporters with unreasonable and required financial support ("donations") to the financial needs of the church, which often includes a personal, financial lifestyle change of the leadership. Not every leader fits this category, but there are some who takes advantage of churches and groups to boost their own personal well-being.

The term **"spiritual abuse"** was coined in the late twentieth century to refer to alleged misuse and abuse of authority by church leaders. Lambert defines spiritual abuse as "a type of psychological predomination that could be rightly termed — religious enslavement. He further identifies "religious enslavement" as being a product of what is termed in the Bible "witchcraft," or "sorcery." (Lambert, 1996)

## Abusive Churches are identified through five categories:

1. <u>Authority and Power</u> - abusive groups misuse and distort the concept of spiritual authority. Abuse arises when leaders of a group claim to themselves power and authority that lacks the dynamics of open accountability and the capacity to question or challenge decisions made by leaders. The shift demands moving from general respect for an office bearer to one where members loyally submit without any right to disagree.

2. <u>Manipulation and Control</u> - abusive groups are characterized by social dynamics where fear, guilt, and threats are routinely used to produce unquestioning obedience, group conformity, and stringent tests of loyalty to the leaders are

demonstrated before the group. Biblical concepts of the leader-disciple relationship tend to develop into a hierarchy where the leader's decisions control and usurp the disciple's right or capacity to make choices on spiritual matters or even in daily routines of what form of employment, form of diet and clothing are permitted.

3. <u>Elitism and Persecution</u> - abusive groups represent themselves as unique and have a strong organizational tendency to be separate from other bodies and institutions; independent or separate, with diminishing possibilities for internal correction and reflection.

4. <u>Life-style and Experience</u> - abusive groups foster rigidity in behavior and in belief that requires unswerving conformity to the group's ideals and social traditions.

5. <u>Dissent and Discipline</u> - abusive groups tend to suppress any kind of internal challenges and dispute concerning decisions made by leaders. Acts of discipline may involve emotional and physical humiliation, physical violence or removal, acute and intense acts of punishment for arguments and disobedience.

I found out through research that there are eight

characteristics of spiritual abuse, and some of these overlap. They are listed for you so you don't have to be confused about spiritual abuse and how to identify it.

1. Charisma and pride,
2. Anger and intimidation,
3. Greed and fraud,
4. Immorality,
5. Enslaving authoritarian structure,
6. Exclusivity,
7. Demanding loyalty and honor, and
8. New revelation.

These characteristics can easily be identified in any churches, groups, or structures that aim at controlling its members beyond what the Bible has set forth. Knowing all this, why would someone want to be spiritually abused? We have so many people in the church being abused because they are disassociated with who they are, what they feel, and who is in control of their lives. They are separated from their sexuality, feelings, needs, and love for God, therefore it's easy to allow someone else to control their minds and emotions.

I remember growing up in the church and  the first Sunday of every month was communion Sunday. I watched at the end of every  service how everyone would leave except the middle age and older people of the church. No young people were allowed to take communion, being that we didn't understand the meaning of what communion was all about. I stopped leaving church and stayed for communion after I accepted Christ. People stared at me and wondered why I was there. I felt stupid, but  I kept taking communion until other young people started remaining after services, too. There were so many taboos in the church.

As I grew older, I took note of many ungodly actions being allowed to filter through the church by the pastor and leaders, with no harness or corrections made concerning it. I remember that it was acceptable to have extra marital affairs in the church, babies by other members' spouses, steal money from the collection plates, and food from pantry and church events. You were warned to keep it to yourself or be shunned by the culprits.

The hurt and harm from spiritual abuse is not always intentional. Most Christians who abuse others are sincere, believe they are obeying the

Bible, and are convinced they are being led by God to do what they do. Sometimes, they focus on being big and well known among others or on some great vision or work, until they're not aware or don't notice abuse being applied to the members. With abusive leaders, there are no doubts, questions, or comments allowed in their presence that will shine light on them. They are always right, they're always the super spiritual one, they love God more than others, they're the best and only right church, everyone else is wrong about what they believe and stand for. Whenever someone disagrees with them, then they feel you are disagreeing with the God that told them to abuse you. Most abusive leaders have exchanged some type of personal addiction for a spiritual addiction that calls for no accountability to anyone and is beyond correction.

## Confront action of others

How do we protect God's people from the toxic influences of an intoxicated leader or others in authority? When abuse is not reported, the abused is enabling the abuser and harboring a fugitive from being helped. We have been taught to keep our mouths shut and keep the peace.

The church's role should be to help, not hurt the

offender, motivating him or her to repent of the sin committed and return to the fellowship of the church. We must be honest with ourselves and others. We are our brothers' keeper. We must forgive and restore one another. The time for refreshing the body of Christ keeps passing by because we are not willing to change our attitude and behavior. Church is becoming a mockery. Outside people laugh and scoff at how we don't love one another, don't get along, and can't fellowship with other churches outside our own beliefs, yet we declare we're on our way to heaven. Not going to happen.

The Bible even tells us if our brother offends us, how to approach the situation and get it right with them. We tend to live in denial of all wrongdoings and pretend to be so holy until it hurts and hampers the growth and development of the next church generations. My mom used to call it "the pot calling the kettle black." Finding fault outside of one's self is the easy way out without repenting. Admitting the church has fallen short and want to be renewed will stop spiritual abuse in its tracks. Try forgiveness for a change instead of knit picking, love in place of hatred, humility instead of pride, compliments without jealousy.

Jesus died that we could have abundant life and that life is in Him, not us. We have to replace Christ as Lord of our lives, and not Savior only so we can handle his people with unconditional love.

# THE SHEPHERD'S ROLE
## Chapter Two

---◦◦◦---

*T*he role of the leader / under-shepherds is to lead people to the Great Shepherd, Jesus Christ, and teach them how to be His disciples, in submission to Him and His authority. Hyper-spiritual leaders, instead, lead people to themselves, and indoctrinate them to be their followers, in total submission to them and their authority. In essence, these dominating shepherds teach that they are the church-members' lord, master, and savior, rather than Christ. They indoctrinate members to believe that the <u>spiritual leaders of the church themselves</u> are the members' "spiritual covering" (a totally false and unbiblical concept), and any member who ever leaves the church will be "out from under" their "covering," be without any covering or what they call, "uncovered," and will experience terrible curses and other horrible consequences as a result. Fear tactics are implemented to scare congregants from leaving the church. From the pulpit, "crazy and bazaar stories" are exaggerated about what happened to persons or families who were so spiritually rebellious, who left the church without the blessings and approval of their "spiritual authority." A performance-based approval and promotion system keeps members in internal turmoil and fear as they jump through all the hoops the spiritual taskmasters put before them, in an attempt to seek their leaders' approval and favor. These constant violations of the church result in members living under a threat of being bullied by leaders and those in charge of organizations, committees, and associations.

I have a fresh sense of bullying in the pulpit mentality from growing up attending a Pentecostal church. I remember many times the pastor getting up in the pulpit and embarrassing the members for not being able to give extra offerings, specials during certain events and donations to their own personal causes. Some choir directors and singers were told not to participate in certain services unless they paid certain amounts of money. Others were coerced by verbal means from the pulpit to line up and pay, causing them to lose homes, cars, and get behind in household bills. There were times when the pastor would chastise or intimidate the members in front of guests to ensure he/she acknowledged his/her authority and position as head of the church. This should never happen in the house of God. Other times, leaders have made the members to feel like slaves or oxen with heavy weights on, trying to fulfill roles not even identified in the Bible. The Scripture states, "Whom the Son set free is free indeed." This is a deception from the enemy. Satan uses whoever submits to his tactics to try and destroy the Lord's churches. The Bible says in John 10:10a "that the thief came to kill, steal, and destroy. We must avoid the deception that is being presented to the churches today.

We have to fight the enemy with the weapons God told us to use instead of fighting one another.

So fight with the Word:

## 2 CORINTHIANS 10:4-6

*[4] For the weapons of our warfare are not carnal but mighty in God for pulling down strongholds, [5] casting down arguments and every high thing that exalts itself against the knowledge of God, bringing every thought into captivity to the obedience of Christ, [6] and being ready to punish all disobedience when your obedience is fulfilled. (NKJV)*

# AVOIDING DECEPTION
## Chapter Three

---

*W*hat causes someone to become a leader, start a ministry, then begin to control all of its members' lives like they are God? What causes a preacher to want to isolate its members from their families and loved ones? What happens to Christians that accept Jesus as Savior, get filled with the baptism of the Holy Spirit, then walk away from it all, quitting the church, quitting reading and studying the Bible, quitting praying and doing what's right, to eventually end on the couch watching pornography, X-rated television programs, ending up in adultery, molestation, physical abuse, or becoming involved in same sex affairs and activities. These and other questions are running though our minds daily when we see the lives of people so messed up by spiritual abuse. Why would a Christian leave the church and try to have a relationship without God, and yet blame God for how he/she turns out? It is called deception.

Deception is believing what is false or invalid to be true, misrepresentation of the facts, being enticed to do wrong, misled by false information, to be fooled by others, dishonesty and deceit. It is falling away from the things of God, yet appearing to be faithful and still on track. Whenever someone leaves God and goes in the opposite direction, they are open to deception in any manner it comes.

In the New Testament, the Bible warns us not to be deceived. We are living in the last days, and even the very elect of God will be deceived if they don't stay in right relationship with the Lord. I'm talking about strong churches, strong members, consistent prayer warriors, and Word walkers. People will be deceived and walk away when they get out of the Word, stop praying, stop giving, and keep right relationships.

According to the Scriptures:

2 TIMOTHY 3:13

[13] *In fact, evil men and false teachers will **become worse and worse**, deceiving many, they themselves having been deceived by Satan. It's happening all over America today. (TLB)*

ISAIAH 60:1-3

*Arise, my people! Let your light shine for all the nations to see!
For the glory of the Lord is streaming from you. ²Darkness as black
as night shall cover all the peoples of the earth, but the glory of the
Lord will shine from you. ³All nations will come to your light;
mighty kings will come to see the glory of the Lord upon you. (TLB)*

We still have opportunity to fix this mess.
Spiritual abuse doesn't have to run rampant
throughout our churches.

## 2 THESSALONIANS 2:1-3

*And now, what about the coming again of our Lord Jesus Christ and
our being gathered together to meet him? Please don't be upset and
excited, dear brothers, by the rumor that this day of the Lord has
already begun. If you hear of people having visions and special
messages from God about this, or letters that are supposed to have
come from me, don't believe them. 3 Don't be carried away and
deceived regardless of what they say. For that day will not come
until two things happen: first, **there will be a time of great rebellion
against God**, and then the man of rebellion will come—the son of
hell. (TLB)*

Looking at our churches today, we have been
convinced to believe that every prophetic word
spoken over us and about us must be true, since it
comes from the leader. Not necessarily true.
There are false prophets and leaders that have
entered the ministry for gain sake and not to
bring people to salvation and reconciliation.

Instead, the love that we should be exhibiting in the church is so cold and indifferent.

## MATTHEW 24:12

*Sin will be rampant everywhere and will cool the love of many. (TLB)*

1 Peter 5:8-9 (TLB)

Be careful—**watch out for attacks from Satan,** your great enemy. He prowls around like a hungry, roaring lion, looking for some victim to tear apart. 9 Stand firm when he attacks. Trust the Lord; and remember that other Christians all around the world are going through these sufferings too.

"Many are the afflictions of the righteous, but the Lord delivers us out of them all," is a Scripture that's repeated daily by the church, and is used to enslave members to remain silent against spiritual abuse, believing they have to endure afflictions. Spiritual abuse should not be a **"church affliction."**

It is not that easy to avoid deception. There was a time when a pastor made a statement and you could "**take it to the bank**", so to speak. Now, there are very few credible leaders in the church, but there are still some great leaders and pastors out there doing and saying what's right and treating people right. Not every leader or pastor is crooked or abusive, some really love God and people. On the other hand, many leaders or people in authority have adopted the spirit of lying to its members about issues of the church and matters of the heart. They hide church information from the congregation and only reveal it to the crew, the posse, the yes men and women, the ones who go along with the crookedness and wrong doings, even to the extent of bonding them and making members swear not to reveal the truth to anyone who asks. It makes it hard to leave or break ties with the inner circle in the church when these rules have been tacked on to your other duties as a member or other leader in any church. You desire to do what's right, but have sold your soul to the enemy. The carnal mind leads you to believe they are right and would not hurt the body of Christ or ask you to do something contrary to the Word of God, after all, they are called of God.

Spiritual abuse represents a cliché often used in the church, "whitewashed tombs"- being one way on the outside and another way inside. Spiritual abuse is a power struggle of higher powers wanting more power. Why spiritual abuse over and over?

People tend to move toward what they already know and accept it as the truth or what they are familiar with, even when they see it renders unhealthy relationships. A good example is a woman who marries an alcoholic and swears that it will never happen again, yet she marries another alcoholic later on in life. The known becomes comfortable.

There are many major types of abuses that we talk about and have been able to create organizations in our society to deal with and provide help to the person in need, but the church is not seen as having a need in these areas, yet many members have committed suicide, killed others, started a drinking binge, relinquished their lives to drugs and other forms of habits, including losing their sanity. They have been raped, molested, sodomized, and sexually assaulted by leaders in the church, yet they report nothing to the authorities, because the church doesn't tell its business to the world system. The next chapter gives examples of types of abuses we encounter and descriptions of what those abuses look and sound like.

# MAJOR TYPES OF SPIRITUAL ABUSE
Chapter Four

———◦◦◦———

## What is Emotional/Verbal Abuse?

Emotional abuse includes non-physical behaviors such as threats, insults, constant monitoring or "checking in," excessive texting, humiliation, intimidation, isolation or stalking.

1. Calling you names and putting you down
2. Yelling and screaming at you.
3. Intentionally embarrassing you in public.
4. Preventing you from seeing or talking with friends and family.
5. Telling you what to do and wear.
6. Stalking you and showing up uninvited. Send you unwanted text messages, letters, emails and voicemails. Constantly call you and hang up.
7. Threatening to expose you to keep you from leaving them.
8. Threatening to harm you or people you care about.

9.  Making you feel guilty or immature when you don't consent to sexual activity.

## What is Financial Abuse?

Financial abuse can be very subtle -- telling you what you can and cannot buy or requiring you to share control of your bank accounts. At no point does church or any group have the right to use your money or tell you how to spend it to control you.

Placing your paycheck in their account and denying you access to it because you need help.

Keeping you from seeing shared bank accounts or records.

Forbidding you to work or limiting the hours you do so you won't miss church.

Preventing you from leaving church without giving large sums of money

Displaying amounts of funding you have given on the wall or in a handout.

Telling you to bring your check stubs to church to prove what the tithes is.

Getting you fired by harassing you, your employer or coworkers on the job.

Hiding or stealing money from outside financial support (grants, loans, wills, etc.).

Using members' social security numbers to obtain credit without permission.

Keeping you from knowing what's in the church accounts or telling you that it's not your business to know what's in the treasury.

Using their money to overpower you because they know you are not in the same financial situation as they are. Boasting about what they have compared to you.

**What is Physical Abuse?**

Physical abuse is any intentional and unwanted contact with you or something close to  your body. Sometimes abusive behavior does not cause pain or even leave a bruise, but  it's  still unhealthy. Examples of physical abuse are:

Scratching, punching, biting, strangling or kicking.

Throwing something at you such as a phone, book, Bible, or hymnal.

Pulling your hair or slapping your face.

Pushing or pulling you.

Grabbing your face to make you look at them.

Grabbing you to prevent you from leaving or to force you to go somewhere.

## What is Sexual Abuse?

Sexual abuse refers to any action that pressures or coerces someone to do something sexually they don't want to do. It can also refer to behavior that impacts a person's ability to control their sexual activity or the circumstances in which sexual activity occurs, including oral sex, rape or restricting access to birth control and condoms.

Unwanted kissing or touching.

Sexual contact with someone who is very drunk, drugged, unconscious or otherwise unable to give a clear and informed "yes" or "no."

Threatening someone into unwanted sexual activity.

Repeatedly pressuring someone to have sex or perform sexual acts.

Repeatedly using sexual insults toward someone.

Rape or attempted rape.

Forcing yourself on the members of the

congregation in sexual relations against their will and impregnating them.

Touching boys and girls in inappropriate areas and daring them to tell someone

I'm aware of so many episodes of young people who have been taken advantage of by pastors and leaders in the church, but the church swept it under the rug.

## What is Digital Abuse?

Digital abuse is the use of technologies such as texting, sexting, and social networking to bully, harass, stalk or intimidate a member/group. In a healthy relationship, all communication is respectful whether in person, online or by phone. It is never ok for someone to do or say anything that makes you feel bad, lowers your self-esteem or manipulates you.

Tells you who you can or can't be friends with on Facebook and other sites.

Sends you negative, insulting or even threatening emails, Facebook messages, tweets, or other messages online.

Uses sites like Facebook, Twitter, Instagram and

others to keep constant tabs on you.

Sends you unwanted, explicit pictures and demands you send some in return.

Constantly texts you and makes you feel like you can't be separated from your phone for fear that you will be punished.

Searches through your phone frequently, checks up on your pictures, texts and outgoing calls.

## Anger/Emotional Abuse

Anger/emotional abuse is found everywhere. There's no excuse for anyone to use anger or emotional abuse to get what they want, and it's never your fault if they do. You might think that if you just change the way you are that you can fix any relationship -- but sometimes no matter what you do, the other person / persons won't change.

Also, remember you have options. You have the right to be in a safe and healthy relationship and the right to end an unhealthy one, whether physical or spiritual. It may not be easy to break up with a controlling partner or church, so alert someone else if you need to talk about it. Don't let anger and emotional issues build up inside you. Deal with the problem and get help immediately. Prolonged anger hurts everyone, not just you. Stop the enemy from having a hay day with God's people.

Examples of anger / emotional abuse are:

> ➢ Putting you down
> ➢ Making you feel bad about yourself
> ➢ Name calling
> ➢ Making you think you're crazy
> ➢ Playing mind games
> ➢ Humiliating you
> ➢ Making you feel guilty

There are many other forms of abuse that are out there, but won't be directly discussed in detail in this book, but they are real. They are: abuse of power, abuse of rank, alcohol abuse, animal abuse, dating abuse, drug abuse, employee abuse, gay abuse, legal abuse, medical abuse, nursing abuse, parental abuse, patient abuse, police abuse, political abuse, prison abuse, racial abuse, self-abuse, sibling abuse, societal abuse, spousal abuse, teacher abuse, telephone abuse, and workplace abuse just to name a few. Many of the above-named abuses also reflect on past experiences with leaders in church, public, and private sectors. Because of being hurt by church folks, laypersons have gone out into society and applied the same types of abuses on others. Hurting people hurt people, a saying we consistently hear and repeat, in fact, it is true.

# SPIRITUAL ABUSE TOWARDS A LEADER
## Chapter Five

What happens when a congregation impose spiritual abuse upon its leader? This happens daily in the church, especially in churches that have staff, deacons, trustees, and other groups that govern the church or are allowed to run the church. It could be families that give the largest amounts of money, been a part of the church for the longest period of time, or groups that everyone is afraid of because of their domination, manipulation, and intimidation. A story I remember growing up was when an elderly mother of the church told my mother to move out of her seat. She had been sitting there for years when my mom sat in her seat on the pew. She was very rude, but my mother moved to keep down confusion with the family, long time members of the congregation. Wow! What a way to start church.

I've also seen abusers in the church call all inactive members to show up at conferences to vote against the leader, pastor or whoever was in authority. People don't have to be in authority to be abusive. You have rude, nasty ushers, disrespectful deacons, misguided musicians, obnoxious greeters, among other abusive forces in churches. Power and authority have gone to their heads and ruled out what should come from their hearts such as love, compassion, kindness, and patience. Many times when members disagree with leaders or authority, they become hostile and intimidating, enforcing their power and positions against leadership to get the leader or authoritative figure to yield to their demands. Many great or promising pastors have been fired, released, or even ignored because of spiritual abuse of other people or groups in the church.

If you experience an abuser as acting on the behalf of God's stead, you need to speak up and clear the air of any misconceptions you have without fear of being rebuked or embarrassed. This doesn't happen most of the time because people have been told that "obedience is better than sacrifice", in other words, open your mouth against them and you will be sacrificed. So you bow down and become afraid to speak up and too fearful to leave the church. You have been told that if you leave, something bad will happen to you. It's a lie straight from the pits of hell to keep you in bondage. Even leaders and pastors have a right to leave a church that will not change.

Well, what about the preacher that wants to leave, but can't? They remain in abusive situations because of the friendships they've made, the money they're paid, the lifestyle they enjoy. They sacrifice their wives, husbands, children and family to please the church and the abusers. They tell others about their hurt and pain, but can't commit to leaving it all behind. They also stay because they have invested so much time, skills, and manpower into teaching, preaching, and training others to be like Christ. It feels like going from something to nothing if you leave.

This puts pressure on pastors and leaders and we read about them in the news, on Facebook, and in magazines committing suicide, promiscuity, unnatural affections, adultery, and other illegal activities right through the church. They don't have anyone they feel like they can trust to help them through the abuse. Oh, yeah, preachers get abused, too. It becomes tiring reading about the multitude of preachers leaving the ministry because of the pressure of the congregation and the abuse that they can't break free from. Pastors die spiritually, too.

There is so much statistics about pastors and depression, burnout, health, low pay, spirituality, relationships and longevity—and none of them are good. According to the Schaeffer Institute, here are some statistics that we need to take a close look at.

| | |
|---|---|
| 90% | Fatigued and worn out |
| 89% | Have considered leaving the ministry |
| 81% | No discipleship or mentoring classes |
| 77% | Don't have good marriages |
| 75% | Poorly trained in ministry |
| 72% | Only study Bible when preparing a sermon |
| 71% | Burned out and fighting depression |
| 70% | Don't have close, personal friends |
| 63% | Have been fired from pastoral positions |
| 50% | Divorced or in the process of a divorce |
| 40% | Have had outside affairs or affairs with church members |
| 31% | Dropped out of the ministry altogether |
| 26% | Actually have personal devotions |
| 25% | Membership attends Bible study |
| 23% | Happy with who they are in Christ, at church, and at home |

This is not true of all pastors and leaders in the church. There are many who are excellent in obeying their call, pastoring great churches, and managing their own personal family lives as well. Christ is still the MAIN THING in Ministry. Outside of that, we get in trouble with the leadership roles in the church. It's time to change the statistics. Time to let Satan know we're not falling for the traps anymore.

##  2 CORINTHIANS 10:4

*For the weapons of our warfare are not carnal, but mighty through God to the pulling down of strong holds.*

A s Christians, we are not alert to the tactics of Satan, even though we boast about fighting and winning. We get so caught up into ministry, gifts, giving, conferences, and people that the enemy has already wreaked havoc in our homes, churches, ministries, and families. Exposing Satan is more than being in the prayer line, laying on of hands, and being anointed with oil. I've seen many people experience being slain in the spirit, to rise up from the floor and be defeated once again by Satan. The Bible says, Satan disguises himself as an angel of light (I John 5:19) therefore we must be alert at all times. Many church leaders and Pastors are led by Satan to hide behind their pulpits, robes, chains, and vestures as they deliberately abuse the body of Christ. God is not pleased with this type of behavior.

The leaders/pastors use phrases such as "the Lord told me to tell you or I got a Word from God for you because we are too lazy to seek God    for ourselves or develop the gifts in us. I'm rather tired of people lying on God. There are some true Words for the body of Christ out there by true leaders/ pastors, but can't we stop running to church and behind conferences for just a "Word". There are 66 books in the Bible full of Words. All we have to do is open it, read it, pray over the understanding, apply it, and then live in the manifestations of it. It's just that simple. We need to consult God about our own lives and follow what He says to do, which is believe not every spirit, but try the spirits.

## I JOHN 4:1

*Beloved, believe not every spirit, but try the spirits whether they are of God: because many false prophets are gone out into the world.*

All God wants leaders to do is preach the Word in season and out of season and exactly as He instructs them to; no more or less. It's time out for sugar-coating, watering down, and putting honey on the Word to catch lost souls. The Word doesn't need you to change someone, it changes people lives by itself. We must remember that pastors and leaders are held to a higher standard and

Satan enjoys seeing them fall, die prematurely, commit sins, and turn their backs on God. Satan knows that if he can get the leaders and pastors to turn their backs on God, it's a piece of cake to trick the congregation to do the same thing. How dumb we are to allow Satan and his demons to have such power over our lives like this. We have to stop fighting each other and turn on and fight the real enemy, Satan. The worst part is we know better.

## The Common Tactics of the devil

There are at least 4 common tactics of the enemy that shows up consistently. We are so smart to recognize what's wrong with each other that we fail to recognize the trick of the enemy. So, I'm going to school you today as to what they are so we won't continue to be ignorant toward his devices.

**Deception-** Jesus told us that the devil is a liar and the Father of lies in John 8, but we still listen to his empty promises. He has bewitched us through code switching (moving back and forth between two dialogues) and wordsmithing (working with words skillfully). To name just a few, what used to be called abortion is now called choice, sodomy is now referred to as gay, fornication is labeled co-habitation, and God doesn't agree with any of it. Satan has tricked the church in to calling good, bad and bad, good. It's time to wake up and called sin what it is, SIN.

**Division-** John 17:22 begins by saying that Jesus wants us to be one just as He and the Father are one. Satan's plans are to cause so much division in the church among leaders and members that we won't get along with each other or other churches outside of ourselves. We run around thinking and teaching that we are the only true church. Well, I got news for you 'Elijahs' you're not the only ones that have not bowed down. God has a remnant of people that will serve Him, regardless of the circumstances. There is so much tension in the church until it gets more attention than God's Word. Trust me, I have hardly been able to tell someone I was writing about spiritual abuse without them wanting to share their story. Anger, pride, greed, fears, misunderstandings, and mistakes have lent themselves to the division among God's people. Every church trying to be bigger and better than the other one. Why?

We all share a common enemy, Satan himself, but

would rather blame one another than to put the blame where it belongs, on the rightful owner, Satan.

**Diversion**- The devil is always trying to turn the church away from its calling- to win souls for Christ. Loving God with all our hearts, mind, and soul and loving our neighbors as ourselves is becoming a pastime. We're so distracted by the lust of the world, the lust of our flesh and the pride of life until we don't have time to read, study, or pray. The enemy easily diverts  our focus from what God has to  say to what the world and others think and say. We're caught up in the fear of the recent killings in our nation, flooding and fires in our cities, sex-trafficking in the land, and brutality of man vs. police officers that we can't attend to or thing on the things that are pure, lovely, true, honest, just, or of good report. Stop allowing your attention to be all over the place and bring your mind into captivity to the Word of God.

**Discouragement**- The place I found myself many times after battling issues with church agendas and leaders who refuse to lead in the ways of truth. The poison of discouragement  has rampaged the church in such a way that the saints are giving up on holiness. I'm not talking about long skirts and the likes, that's foolishness, but about living a life pleasing unto God without offense. Back in the former days, it was holiness or hell. They didn't know a lot of the Word, but they knew they could not be saved or called a Christian living the same old life.

Satan tires us out, overwhelms us , limits our resources, and stunts our growth, while delivering blow after blow to a lazy, superstitious, defiant, and confused generation of people who are supposed to be preparing the next generation to meet God.

The enemy has found out that if he can break your will to fight, he will own you. If the enemy can wear you down and take your strength, he can control you. If he can get you divided against one another, he can take the city. What are we thinking? In Saint Matthews 12: 25, Jesus states,

"Every kingdom divided against itself is brought to desolation." That is exactly what the enemy is doing now, destroying, churches, ministries, marriages, relationships, families, homes, and friendships. I was told many times when people left a church not to have anything more to do with them.

The court system is even changing the laws to fit ungodliness at an alarming rate. Lawsuits are being filed against the church to legislate their actions, to withdraw their tax-exemptions, to mandate what can or can't be preached from the pulpit, what areas a church can be built in according to zoning rules, increasing television costs to get the gospel out of the homes, and exposing leaders and pastors as scrutiny to the entire world so the gospel can be stopped. Instead of us fighting Satan's tactics, we sit around and discuss which televangelist we don't like, which preachers we don't believe in, what the churches should not learn about, especially the prosperity messages, while waking up every morning religiously broke, busted, and disgusted.

What has happened to the church is that it has inherited wolves in sheep clothing that have the wrong appetites, therefore food, sex drives, greed, and sinful lifestyles have taken over. It used to be miracles, healings, blessings, and spiritual growth as the subjects to praise God about. Now we are full of members, but barely making ends meet in our churches today. Being a blessing to others has now turned to "I'm the

other" in need, bless me.

This is why it is vitally important to know the Word of God for yourself. You are fearfully and wonderfully made. Never let the enemy downplay your relationship with Christ and others. Stop letting him destroy you. Recognize his tactics and use the armor of God to combat his forces.

The Bible records other devices that Satan uses. If you look through the Old and New Testaments. You will find the recording of how Satan has brought many people down. Stop being ignorant of his devices. Know the enemy. Learn his ways. Be able to see him coming from miles away. God has left us the Holy Spirit to help us maintain prevention against the attacks of the enemy. You have to know how the devil operates. Satan already know that the seasoned saints know how to avoid alcohol, drugs, sexual addictions, promiscuity, pornography, and fleshly sins, but he has retrained the lustful desires in unforeseen ways that you wouldn't imagine. The very ones that you look up to, respect highly, and honor the most are breaking records on television, in the newspaper, on the internet, and on social media and in other publications that expose them asoutright sinners, preaching one thing and living another.

## FREEDOM FROM ABUSES
### Chapter Seven

divider ornament

$\mathscr{H}$ow do we get free from abuses that have left scars in our lives?

By working the Word of God (the Scriptures) in our lives.

Is there life, Christian faith and spiritual peace after coming out of the Baptist, Catholic, Charismatic, Holiness, Methodist, A.M.E, C.M.E., United Methodist, Non-denominational, Pentecostal, Jehovah's Witnesses, Seventh Day Adventist, Islamic, Buddhist, the Hindu Church or any other church? Yes, there is, but it won't be easy or quickly diffused. There will be a period of time when the person coming out will be like the "man with no spiritual family, a loner." Life will be confusing, and one's spiritual comfort zone will be exceedingly strained. Will it be worth it? Yes, Lord, yes! Perhaps these words will help comfort you and give you energy as you make the journey toward becoming free or free again.

The worst positions to be in is having envy, jealousy, strife, bitterness, unforgiveness, resentment, pride, and hatred in your heart for anyone, whether in the body of Christ or not. These areas are known as spiritual viruses in the church that must be stamped out at all cost. Remaining in a spiritually abusive situation will leave you in a place where love is hard to find, love is hard to receive, and love is hard to give away. Because of its destructive power, spiritual abuse can be a fatal attraction. A fatal attraction is something that draws people into lust and enticement, which when adhered to, brings about death and spiritual separation from God. God never uses evil to tempt man. **James 1:13, 14** says, *" Let no man say when he is tempted, I am tempted of God: for God cannot be tempted with evil, neither tempteth he any man. But every man is tempted, when he is drawn away of his own lust, and enticed."* When we are enticed, we are drawn away from God to committing sin and violating the laws of God.

Sin operates the same way the Word of God does. We hear it, believe it, receive it and accept it. So instead of giving place to the devil, we need to be breaking free from the results of spiritual abuse and returning back to the Father, our first love. You have to purpose in your heart to live pure and Holy, fill your life with God's Word, avoid every appearance of evil, keep your focus on Christ and not man, and submit yourself to God- resist the devil and he will flee from you. We resist everything else, now it's time to actually work the Word in our lives. Getting free is possible and God wants you free. It doesn't take a rocket scientist to see that the enemy has taken a powerful effect on millions of God's people. It's time to renounce every work of darkness and every spiritual attack that has caused us to be spiritually abused and move forward in a new and exciting relationship with the Lord.

Coming out is no easy task, but it is possible. If you are one of those who are coming out, I wish to assure you that you can survive with your spirituality and faith intact. In the end, you will find a new love for the Lord Jesus, a new appreciation for his church, and a new compassion for those who have not yet understood his love and grace. There will be dangers, of course. Some are internal, such as the repeated danger of anger, hatred and bitterness. Others are external, such as the superficiality of much that comes under the guise of Christianity.

Be patient with yourself. Trust in God. Turn your life over to Him again. Ask God to direct your paths. Keep your focus.

We heal as we reveal. We change as we rearrange. We reverse as we rehearse.

When you share, you must confront the abuser and the abused situation.

Your sharing what happen to you will help:

a) reach the person who don't know God but wants a chance to
b) reach the person who walked away from God only to regret it
c) reach the person who wants to return to God, but thinks he/she can't
d) reach the person who is on the brink of suicide, murder, drugs, alcoholism, etc. to have a change of mind
e) reach the person who thought they must keep quiet and never break the unspoken rules of the church
f) reach the person who dreams of enjoying a great relationship with Christ

Hiding the truth destroys you, others, and the church.

**James 5:16** tells us to *confess our faults one to another and pray for one another that ye may be healed, the effectual fervent prayer of a righteous man availeth much.*

# CONFRONTING SPIRITUAL ABUSE
## Chapter Eight

———◦◦◦◦———

*T*he time is long overdue for the Church to start talking about and confronting spiritual abuse. It is no secret anymore. Everyone knows it's happening, but they're just too ashamed to admit it.

We have to stop pretending that it does not take place in our churches and face the truth that even we ourselves may have been abusive to members or even tried to control, manipulate, dominate, others' lives. In talking with people from all walks of life, all other races of people, and other religions, it has been established that spiritual abuse is real and happens on a consistent basis in most of our churches.

Don't believe me, just ask some of these churches that have had splits. The thing that caused the split and pushed members to leave resulted from some type of abuse allowed in the church, resulting in differences of opinions and no solutions acceptable by all.

Spiritual abuse is like other types of abuse, but

it's committed under the banner of spirituality. It can be subtle or painfully loud—anything from unquestioned pastoral authority, to practices of shaming members if they don't fulfill religious expectations, to badmouthing members who have left.

Recently, former pastors of mega churches, televangelist, and over 400 pastors have resigned from ministries due to infidelity and adultery. They have given us prime examples of what forms of spiritual abuse can look like. Former church members have accused preachers of a variety of abuse, including forcing women to get abortions and men to get vasectomies. However, other leaders' misuse of handling the church and its funds with a self-admitted domineering spirit is a type of abuse that can be found tucked away in many of our churches. Many preachers' wives have had to live through hell at home while defending an abuser, their leader, pastor and husband. The children grow up with hatred in them towards God for allowing their parents to be so mean and evil towards them, yet portraying another person or image in front of the congregation.

Spiritual abuse can be subtle or painfully apparent—anything from throwing "shade" in the pulpit, to making comparisons between members who don't follow orders, to spreading confidential information to the congregation,, to setting members down and stripping positions from those who don't agree with the plans or program.

It's fair to say an overwhelming majority of Christians have experienced some variation of spiritual abuse; so have I. It took me years to acknowledge that what I had experienced in my childhood years and even later in life was indeed spiritually abusive. The first time I used that term, I felt crazy and kind of afraid. Why was this happening to me? Church should not be like this. Oh, but it was, and worse.

Then I started watching the little things that kept happening to me because I disagreed or had my own ideas and thoughts about a thing. Members stopped speaking to me, treated me as if I had a disease, and even spread lies about me. When confronting the pastor, he/she always made me feel like I was making up something, or I was the guilty person, and had caused whatever transpired upon myself. In other words, it was my fault. Ever felt that way? You don't have to be guilty to feel guilty. Faults will be laid upon your shoulder, and if you don't speak up and deny them, everyone will believe the lies about you. I've endured years of lies, trickery, hypocrisies, and the sort, but God kept me through it all. When nights were long and dark, I remember praying about situations and crying myself to sleep. I've covered up a lot of wrong doings through the years of my Christian walk because I was taught that love covers a multitude of sin and that we don't have the rights to expose leaders. Quotes from the Bible like *"they are not your servants"* kept me tied up in knots many times in the church, when sinful acts were committed and I should have spoken up. I am so glad to be free from the hurt and pain of those moments of the past. Christ died to bring me back to the Father, but I was so in love with being validated by others until I became blind to the truth. I thought it was great to be the loudest praiser, best singer, the coolest and most liked person in the church, but it didn't keep me from being abused by leaders. You probably feel the same way. You've done your best to obey and be faithful, but it's never enough. Declare yourself not guilty now. You've been used, too.

That's the position many Christians are in today. You have been made to believe it's all your fault. You're made to feel that this is a normal situation so you don't seem to see it as an abusive problem at all. I would have never considered any of my earlier church experiences spiritually abusive if I hadn't awakened from my deep spiritual sleep. I had to back off, separate myself, and investigate my own health and happiness. Why was I sad at times when being a Christian is supposed to be a joyous affair? Why did I want to be alone at times when everyone else seemed to enjoy hanging out together? The questions kept piling up in my mind with no apparent answers. I had to find me, the one I used to know and loved. It was only when I was removed from the situation that I realized that what I had considered normal was actually harming me. I was experiencing abuse and lying about it. NEVER AGAIN!!

Innately, the Church doesn't like to admit when it

has done wrong, which results in its members burying their hurt or leaving. Often, this pain becomes a wedge between God and His people, and I have met many people who have walked away from their faith because it had simply been beaten out of them or too overwhelming to continue in. We were taught that God has not given us a spirit of fear, but we knew not to stand up for what's right, fearing the consequences of being abused and left as a loner among the congregation. Why would you speak out when you know everyone will fight against you and abandon friendship with you, it's easier to just go along and never cross the line.

While physical forms of abuse are easy to condemn, what we need to improve on is recognizing the emotional and psychological abuse. This can be an endless list of things, for instance, deeming certain actions sinful based on church standards rather than biblical principle or questioning the depth of someone's salvation (wearing pants, makeup, jewelry, going to the movies, dancing, head covered, etc.)

The church has imposed so many unscriptural rules and regulations on the body of Christ, based on church made standards and by-laws rather than biblical principles to the point that people don't want to be save anymore, don't want to go to church, and don't want anything to do with God. Prevention is, of course, the best way to address abuse in our churches, and we need to begin the conversation about what that looks like on a practical level. I am by no means an expert on this topic, but I know a few things my church could have done to help address my hurt sooner.

1.  Develop an Openness for Communication

    A major reason of creating an open atmosphere of communication in church is to make sure there are systems of accountability in place for everyone in leadership positions. Allowing a leader to have unquestioned authority over church decisions and policy is a recipe for disaster. Disaster breaks down the principles of God's Word. Along with accountability, there needs to be a willingness for church leadership to listen to congregants. There should never be lack of communication among leaders and members. Everyone should desire to hear and work out any situations that arise among congregants without hostility or abuse.

I would say that many Christians do not feel that there is room to express their honest opinion in their church atmosphere. To address the pain church members may be experiencing, we, the Church need to know what or who is causing it, which means we have to allow the conversation to happen without immediately jumping to the defensive. This could be done in a variety of ways, for instance, appointing someone to receive concerns that members might have—and giving them the authority to really address those concerns.

A simple way is to talk more about the Gospel, spiritual abuse and what grace-filled and loving Christian leadership should look like through sermons, youth activities, Sunday school lessons and Bible studies and prayer services. If grace, truth and forgiveness are common practices and topics of discussion in our churches, then people will be willing to come forward about their own experiences and issues.

## 2. Change the Way You View Things

When we just accept abuse as the norm, we're jeopardizing our lives and putting others in harm's way, thinking we're doing the righteous thing. If it's not broke, don't fix it becomes the attitude of the entire church. Don't discuss anything that will upset the apricot. Well nothing changes until we change. Nothing improves until someone admits there's a problem with the situation at hand. We have to stop believing lies and face the truth. It is what it is. It won't get better until it is addressed and changed.

Look at things from God's perspective. Ask yourself, "What does the Word say about it?" Base your actions and decisions on the Scriptures and not on man-made rules and regulations. Some things are not so serious but we have become so petty in the church. Instead of releasing and letting go, we hold on to conflicts and hold grudges toward people in the church. I had a pastor tell me that he/she was holding on to all the wrong doings of the members to use it against them when the time presented itself. We call that stacking cards. That's what the world does. That type of behavior is unacceptable. View things from a different standpoint, Christ's, and you will never have issues that can't be resolved.

# ARTICLES (Clips) ON SPIRITUAL ABUSE
## Chapter Nine

———◦❊◦———

*Some of the basic spiritual abuse experiences that I've read about include:*

Through the voice of the victims... (the victim' names were omitted)

➢ A leader telling me that even though I was burned out and losing my health, I had to stay in the ministry because if I didn't, I would lose all my gifting to do future ministry.

➢ A church that repeatedly told me they basically had the corner on the market on Jesus and that if we went elsewhere, we would miss God's highest.

➢ A leader who found ministry to be a vehicle for his great gain, lying and manipulating donors to earn more and more money.

➢ A ministry that shamed people into throwing away all my evil music (including jazz, country and western, classical, ballet, etc.!) because they didn't understand the genres of the music industry. They convinced people that all music is evil, except gospel or better known as "church music".

➢ A leader who cornered me, threatened me, and yelled because I brought up a concern that others saw, but would not speak against. This led to panic attacks.

Preachers / leaders often confront sin in others, particularly ones who bring up legitimate biblical issues or they have their circle of influence (inside posse) take on this task, silencing critics.

### Other examples:

Often, we have charismatic leaders at the helm who start off well, but slips into arrogance, and pride. He/she withdraws to a small group of "yes people" and isolates from the needs of others. They become the central figure of the ministry or church believing that without them, the church would collapse.

Members cultivate a dependence on one leader or leaders for spiritual information.

Leaders who demand servant hood of their followers, but live exquisite, expensive lives. They live high above their followers and justify their extravagance as God's favor and approval on their ministry and refer to their members as "the poor people in the church." Unlike Jesus' instructions to take the last seat, they often take the first seat at events and court others to grant them privileges.

➢ Buffers him/herself from criticism by placing people around themselves whose only allegiance is to the leader. Views those who bring up issues as enemies. Sometimes these folks are banished, told to be silent, or shamed into submission.

➢ Leaders who demand that people bow down to them and members believe they are God.

➢ A leader with a competitive spirit who tries to outdo, out sing, out preach, and out pay the other leaders and members, especially re-preaching a message that was already preached well.

➢ A leader that shows favoritism among family and friends, promoting division within the church.

- ➤ Leaders that put financial demands on members who can't afford to give like others, humiliating them by announcing monetary amounts from all members
- ➤ Hold to outward performance but rejects authentic spirituality. Places burdens on followers to act a certain way, dress an acceptable way, and have an acceptable lifestyle.
- ➤ Leaders use exclusivity for allegiance. Followers close to the leader or leaders feel like insiders. Everyone else is on the outside, though they long to be in that inner circle.

Have you ever experienced this kind of situation? What did you do? How did you healed? Did you try to help someone else? What can we do as responsible Christ followers to expose this kind of Satanic abuse? What can we do as leaders to follow in the gentle footsteps of Jesus?

Yet they often confront sin in others, particularly ones who bring up legitimate biblical issues, or they have their circle of influence take on this task.

Still more to come....

These last examples of spiritual abuse came from people that were hurt and are still recovering from the pain it left them. You've read this far, maybe some of these examples have opened old wounds and hurts that you have not addressed yet.

Guilt is the pastor's poison of choice. People always return home from church feeling like they weren't doing enough for the CHURCH... not the Lord. They were jilted into volunteering for ministries and events. People were also made to feel guilty for not having children... and not being married, therefore marriages were arranged and couples ended up with partners they didn't want or was force to make the relationships work. They had to get out... QUICK! Then they were told "God never tells someone to leave a church" by the Pastor. I guess he's the only one who can do that. They are still recovering!

> I can also concur with spiritual abuse in a church I went to many years ago. Amongst many things that were said to me by church leaders (Some, not all) that I felt condemned by, was one of the pastors having a go at me about my competence as

a wife to my abusive husband. I lived in that marriage for almost ten years out of fear that if I left, I was disobeying God and hurting the children emotionally. My ex-husband screamed at our children often, physically, and emotionally bullied my oldest son (his stepson) and the church leaders ignored the abuse. I was only a young Christian at the time, not very knowledgeable on the Word and I put up with it for fear that I was not being a 'good Christian wife' if I ended my marriage! A few years later, my oldest son turned to drugs and alcohol and I almost lost him to suicide on a few occasions, because of the abuse from his stepfather.

➤ I am a survivor of domestic and spiritual abuse. I learned something eye-opening from a Christian ministry that worked with domestic violence. Statistics looked at the vocational choices of those who participated in domestic abuse. The highest numbers went to law enforcement jobs, at all levels. The second highest was pastors. Perhaps this sheds a little light on why there is so much spiritual abuse.

> My first experience with spiritual abuse came about when I disagreed with a pastor over his ultra-conservative position on women. (He wouldn't allow me to make an announcement about an event that I was planning for the church unless my husband stood and introduced me, and stayed beside me to demonstrate his authority over me.) This erupted after I confided in a small group of women leaders about things going on at home. The group included the pastor's wife. I was shamed for putting my abusive husband in bad light. The pastor followed by taking my husband to breakfast and shaming him for not having control over me. He then stripped me of my service in the church.

We were in that inner circle. How scary is that?! It's taken us literally many years after leaving the church itself to really understand who was in the wrong and why. We felt so guilty for even questioning things, disloyal, and if we left, it was like we were leaving God himself. The journey was tremendously painful.

Truthfully, looking back, it was like leaving a cult (even though I was in denial of this for a long time).

> I recently resigned from full time employment with a ministry that reflects in glaring ways to all signs you have listed. I quit when I discovered that the boss had been carrying on sexually for over 8 years with the general manager (30 years his junior) under the guise of a "father-daughter" relationship. My brain and emotions are reeling and feel scarred. I'm counseling with a Christian therapist and didn't realize the deep negative impact my involvement in this ministry was having on me. I'm so thankful God opened my eyes and helped me to get out.

These are just a few of many examples of people who have been abused in the house of God and had to recover from the hurt and damage.

Secrecy may also cloak the area of finances. Pastors may make violent appeals for money, yet offer no assurance that the finances of the church are handled with accountability and integrity.

I have heard that pastors actually tell their congregations that financial decisions of the church do not become a public matter because "the congregation doesn't have the spiritual insight or maturity to understand the dynamics of church finances." Have you heard this line of reasoning?

Some pastors actually preach, *"It doesn't matter what we do with your money. Your responsibility is simply to give."* I don't have an issue with that statement, however, the Bible does commands us to be good stewards -- and part of good stewardship is making sure that proper systems of accountability are established to handle tithes and offerings. **(1 Peter 4:10.)** When the pastor handles the checkbook, writes all the checks, count the monies coming in, and refuse to let the appointed personnel do their job, it becomes apparent that some financial issues need to be reviewed and changed, so that the church won't have future regrets. Some pastors even lock members in the church as a disciplinary measure, pray for only certain people on Sundays, or keep members from being around their own families using threats about what will happen if they miss programs or activities at church. I have friends that have been fired from positions in their church because they would not let the leaders control them or won't side with them against member they don't like.

**Perhaps you have a story to tell, too.** Maybe if you tell your story, you can be released permanently from spiritual abuse and get back in your rightful place in the body of Christ. I can remember many times being intimidated by the pastor in front of my family to make me adhere to being obedient and submissive. I also remember when negative comments were hurled at me to make me fall in line with plans and tactics I knew were not right or part of God's plans for any church. What did I do? I folded under pressure. I buried the hurt so deep until talking about it was far from happening. I pretended that it didn't happen and that the church was okay, loving and kind. I didn't necessarily want to sever the ties that were bound. I knew the day had come and it was time to walk away, but it was almost unbearable to leave and know others would still be abused. It wasn't until something tragic happened to me that I realized if I didn't leave it may be too late later. Every day I asked God to release me from the burden of guilt, enslavement, and the bondage of spiritual abuse. I sought God daily and asked that his will be done in my life. I wanted to be led by God, not people. I had to make a choice between God and man. I didn't have a support system in place that could help me, just mad bashers and condemners. I locked myself up in my house and decided to stay away from people until I could be honest with my own self. I tried to keep in contact with old acquaintances and members, but it didn't work. They had been poisoned and told to stay their distance from me. God answered prayer, though. He will also continue to answer prayer for anyone who needs to be delivered from spiritual abuse. I saw folks who wouldn't even speak to me even though they were the same people I had helped over the years. No matter how I tried to cover it up or lie about it, spiritual abuse had taken place in my life. My new enemy was the church. I couldn't blame God because he had already warned me to get out, but I refused to leave. What a bad decision on my part. It almost destroyed my life. I still think about all the things that have affected me over my past life and I'm so glad God never turned his back on me. I still face challenges, but I'm better equipped to deal with them now and I can help somebody else.

When we look into a mirror, we see someone who

has been abused and don't know how to handle it. We become the victim and eventually the victor over someone else's abusive life. Some people say, *"We are what we eat."* Well, if all you eat is spiritual abuse, over a period of time, you will return the favor upon others. Spiritual abuse begets spiritual abuse. The abuser needs to be forgiven, too. They hurt because  somewhere along the road, if you dig deep, they were abused by someone else in their past and don't know anything else but to pass it on. They're crying for help while committing the abuse. They could get help if we stop lying and pretending that all is well.

# RECOGNIZING A HEALTH CHURCH
## Chapter Ten

————◦◦◦————

*A* healthy church should produce peace and rest for your soul. Establishing healthy spiritual relationships will always be a challenge, but the process will prevent you from becoming weary and worn, trying to jump through religious hoops that promise God's acceptance and love. If, to gain the acceptance of its leaders, your church constantly requires more and more of your life with no end in sight -- and little encouragement along the way -- then you may want to re-examine the church you are attending. Even Jesus went aside to rest.

A healthy church will not allow genuine pastoral concern to cross the line into manipulation or control. A true shepherd will use his influence to draw church members into a close relationship with Jesus, who is the only *"head of the church"* **(Eph. 5:23)**. A true shepherd realizes that the people in his congregation don't belong to him -- they are God's flock.

A healthy church is one who's always reconciling, restoring, and forgiving others. It's a place where everyone is somebody and Jesus is LORD! It's also a place where everyone comes to serve and not be served. Members of healthy churches can strengthen, develop and deepen spiritual relationships, family commitments and communication, marital relationships and covenants, and spiritual values. Real leaders welcome challenges, questions, and comments without reprisals or upheavals. Trusting leaders or pastors will encourage accountability and set up checks and balances that will cause growth in the church and not double standards among the congregation.

Any church that does not have any means of holding a pastor or elder or even a leadership circle accountable for their teaching and their treatment of people is functioning in a non-biblical church governance.

There's a lot of work to be done when it comes to combating spiritual abuse.

- Stop drinking poison and deceiving your own self.
- Scandals should not evolve from the church, just leave and keep the church

in prayer. (touch not God's anointed, which includes others also)

- Don't tear up the church you're leaving, but leave in a rightful manner.
- Disconnect from the sources that abused you until you can deal with them.
- Don't be so quick to believe anything someone says to you about the church or the people you left. Many false rumors and accusations will arise.
- Limit your phone conversations to talk about Christ and his love for the church, not about people. Everyone is looking to gossip with you.
- You are your own worst enemy until you confront your own truth.
- Be bold and strong, trusting God to lead and guide you in the right direction.
- Don't make up any lies about situations that occurred to make you look like the righteous one, just be honest and tell the TRUTH!

**Spiritual Abuse Recovery 101**

The damages caused by spiritual abuse is not irreversible (meaning it can be changed). It's very possible to regain your relationship you had with the Father and build a better one. God's will in your life and the "yes" He wants to say to you is not based on you or what you do, but is based on what Jesus did for you already and what He wants to do in your life now. We serve a God that will not change and makes all things new. God still provides protection, provision, love, peace, healing, deliverance, and his power.

Steps to recovery:

- Understand that you have been wounded-admit your negative feelings-
- admit how you don't trust people or God anymore
- Process what caused the hurt and pain – be honest with your own self speak -the truth and stop pretending nothing happened. Satan loves liars.
- Tell your story- talk about what took place

– find safe leaders / counselors to talk
with-break the don't talk, don't tell rule

- Allow yourself to say no – step down from
positions- don't accept new positions- don't
be pressured to remain-listen to your heart-
grieve your loss- move forward

As you move forward with your life and desire to
continue serving God, build a support group (a
network of Christians) that you can share with or
is available to help others become free from
abuse.

Trust a support system to help you have a safe
place to relax and share. As you do this, you will
be able to trust God again. Talk to others who
have been in the same predicament as you using
the truth you know to dispel lies and deceptions
that has caused you shame and misery. Let your
emotions be expressed through tears and grief,
but don't let the anger, guilt, or fear overtake you.

God is not the group, the inner circle, or the
church. Leaving the church does not mean that
you have left God. Study the attributes and
character of God- He didn't violate you, people
did.

## SPIRITUAL ABUSE TIPS

- ✓ Admit you're being abuse

- ✓ Talk to someone about your spiritual abuse

- ✓ Pray and forgive the abuser and yourself

- ✓ Reconnect your relationship with Christ

- ✓ Find a new church home (if needed) and get involved

- ✓ Follow leaders and pastors as they follow Christ

- ✓ Purpose to be godly examples yourself

- ✓ Teach others how to be a godly example by living it

- ✓ Don't ever put a stumbling block in another person's way

- ✓ Do not destroy the work of God for the sake of people

- ✓ Watch your own self because someone else is watching you

- ✓ Test the spirits to see if they are from God

# SCRIPTURES TO COMBAT SPIRITIAL ABUSE
## Chapter Eleven

━━◦◦◦◦━━

In the Old Testament, God spoke against those who operated in their own authority while abusing the very

people they were to bless. In **Jeremiah 5:30-31,** we read, "*An astonishing and horrible thing has been committed in the land: the prophets prophesy falsely, and the priests rule by their own power; and my people love to have it so.*"(NKJV)

In **Jeremiah 6:13-14**, we read again of self-absorbed prophets and priests who are so preoccupied with their own needs being met that the needs of the people are being ignored. We read: "*From the least of them even to the greatest of them, everyone is greedy for gain, and from the prophet even to the priest everyone deals falsely. And they have healed the brokenness of my people superficially, saying, 'Peace, peace,' but there is no peace*" (NAS).

When He saw the multitudes, "*He was moved with compassion for them, because they were weary and scattered, like sheep having no shepherd*" **(Matt. 9:36).** The Amplified Version expands on the word weary by saying, "*They were bewildered (harassed and distressed and dejected and helpless), like sheep without a shepherd.*"

## ❧ MATTHEW 11:28-30 ☙

[28] Come to Me, all you who labor and are heavy laden, and I will give you rest. [29] Take my yoke upon you and learn from Me, for I am gentle and lowly in heart, and you will find rest for your souls. [30] For my yoke is easy and my burden is light. (NIV)

## ❧ ISAIAH 55:6-7 ☙

[6] Seek ye the Lord while he may be found, call ye upon him while he is near: [7] Let the wicked forsake his way, and the unrighteous man his thoughts: and let him return unto the Lord, and he will have mercy upon him; and to our God, for he will abundantly pardon.

## ❧ PSALM 51:17 ☙

The sacrifices of God are a broken spirit: a broken and a contrite heart, O God, thou wilt not despise.

## ❧ PSALM 103:10-12 ☙

[10] He hath not dealt with us after our sins; nor rewarded us according to our iniquities. [11] For as the heaven is high above the earth, so great is his mercy toward them that fear him. [12] As far as the east is from the west, so far hath he removed our transgressions from us.

## ❧ PSALM 32:5 ☙

I acknowledged my sin unto thee, and mine iniquity have I not hid. I said, I will confess my transgressions unto the Lord; and thou forgavest the iniquity of my sin. Selah.

## ❧ ISAIAH 1:18 ❧

*Come now, and let us reason together, saith the Lord: though your sins be as scarlet, they shall be as white as snow; though they be red like crimson, they shall be as wool. (KJV)*

## ❧ MATTHEW 5:22-24 ❧

*[22] But I say unto you, that whosoever is angry with his brother without a cause shall be in danger of the judgment: and whosoever shall say to his brother, Raca, shall be in danger of the council: but whosoever shall say, Thou fool, shall be in danger of hell fire. [23] Therefore if thou bring thy gift to the altar, and there rememberest that thy brother hath ought against thee; [24] Leave there thy gift before the altar, and go thy way; first be reconciled to thy brother, and then come and offer thy gift. (KJV)*

## ❧ MATTHEW 6:14-15 ❧

*[14] For if ye forgive men their trespasses, your heavenly Father will also forgive you: [15] But if ye forgive not men their trespasses, neither will your Father forgive your trespasses. (KJV)*

## ❧ LUKE 6:27-28 ❧

*But I say unto you which hear, Love your enemies, do good to them which hate you, Bless them that curse you, and pray for them which despitefully use you. (KJV)*

Other references to consider are:

**Acts 3:19, Galatians 6:1-2, Ephesians 1:7-10, Ephesians 4:31-32, Colossians 1:13-14,**

## Colossians 3:13, James 5:16, and I John 1:9

These Scriptures are chosen to help you become free of the guilt and shame the enemy has thrust upon you over the past. Let go and let God free you.

# SCRIPTURES ON FORGIVENESS
## Chapter Twelve

## ❧ EPHESIANS 4:32 ❧

*And be ye kind one to another, tenderhearted, forgiving one another, even as God for Christ's sake hath forgiven you. (KJV)*

## ❧ MARK 11:25 ❧

*And when ye stand praying, forgive, if ye have ought against any: that your Father also which is in heaven may forgive you your trespasses.*

## ❧ LUKE 174:3-4 ❧

*Take heed to yourselves: If thy brother trespass against thee, rebuke him; and if he repent, forgive him.*

## ❧ MATTHEW 6:14 ❧

*For if ye forgive men their trespasses, your heavenly Father will also forgive you:*

## ❧ COLOSSIANS 3:13 ❧

*Forbearing one another, and forgiving one another, if any man have a quarrel against any: even as Christ forgave you, so also [do] ye.*

## ❈ LUKE 6:37 ❈

*Judge not, and ye shall not be judged: condemn not, and ye shall not be condemned: forgive, and ye shall be forgiven:*

## ❈ MATTHEW 18:21-22 ❈

*Then came Peter to him, and said, Lord, how oft shall my brother sin against me, and I forgive him? till seven times?*

## ❈ 1 PETER 3:9 ❈

*Not rendering evil for evil, or railing for railing: but contrariwise blessing; knowing that ye are thereunto called, that ye should inherit a blessing.*

## ❈ PROVERBS 15:1 ❈

*A soft answer turneth away wrath: but grievous words stir up anger.*

## ❈ JAMES 5:16 ❈

*Confess [your] faults one to another, and pray one for another, that ye may be healed. The effectual fervent prayer of a righteous man availeth much.*

## ❈ EPHESIANS 4:31 ❈

*Let all bitterness, and wrath, and anger, and clamour, and evil speaking, be put away from you, with all malice:*

## ❧ MATTHEW 6:12 ❧

*And forgive us our debts, as we forgive our debtors.*

## ❧ PROVERBS 15:18 ❧

*A wrathful man stirreth up strife: but [he that is] slow to anger appeaseth strife.*

## ❧ MATTHEW 6:14 ❧

*For if ye forgive men their trespasses, your heavenly Father will also forgive you:*

## ❧ PHILIPPIANS 4:8 ❧

*Finally, brethren, whatsoever things are true, whatsoever things [are] honest, whatsoever things [are] just, whatsoever things [are] pure, whatsoever things [are] lovely, whatsoever things [are] of good report; if [there be] any virtue, and if [there be] any praise, think on these things.*

## ❧ LUKE 23:34 ❧

*Then said Jesus, Father, forgive them; for they know not what they do. And they parted his raiment, and cast lots.*

## ❧ 1 JOHN 1:9 ❧

*If we confess our sins, he is faithful and just to forgive us [our] sins, and to cleanse us from all unrighteousness.*

## ⊃ 2 CHRONICLES 7:14 ⊂

*If my people, which are called by my name, shall humble themselves, and pray, and seek my face, and turn from their wicked ways; then will I hear from heaven, and will forgive their sin, and will heal their land.*

## ⊃ MATTHEW 18:15 ⊂

*Moreover if thy brother shall trespass against thee, go and tell him his fault between thee and him alone: if he shall hear thee, thou hast gained thy brother.*

## ⊃ JEREMIAH 32:34 ⊂

*And they shall teach no more every man his neighbour, and every man his brother, saying, Know the LORD: for they shall all know me, from the least of them unto the greatest of them, saith the LORD: for I will forgive their iniquity, and I will remember their sin no more.*

## ⊃ MATTHEW 18:21 ⊂

*Matthew 18:21 - Then came Peter to him, and said, Lord, how oft shall my brother sin against me, and I forgive him? till seven times?*

## ⊃ ACTS 2:38 ⊂

*Then Peter said unto them, Repent, and be baptized every one of you in the name of Jesus Christ for the remission of sins, and ye shall receive the gift of the Holy Ghost.*

## Quote on Forgiveness

*A forgiveness should be like a canceled note, torn in two pieces, burned up, so that it can never be shown against a man.* ‡ **Henry Ward Beecher**

Other Scriptures that will help you on your journey to recovery:

### Scriptures on Peace

*Romans 5:1; John 14:27; Isaiah 26:3, 4; Isaiah 57:19-21; Romans 8:6; Philippians 4:6,7*

### Scriptures on Love

*Matthew 5:43-48; John 13:34; Romans 12:9-10; I Corinthians 13:4-7; Galatians 5:13-15; Galatians 6:10; I Peter 1:22; I Peter 4:9-10*

### Scriptures on Forgiving Self

*Psalm 32:1,2,4,5; Psalm 51:1-17; Psalm 103:12; Psalm 130:3,4; Isaiah 55:7; Matthew 6:12; Ephesians 1:7,8; I John 1:9*

### Scriptures on Depression

*Psalm 32; Psalm 42:5-6; 2 Corinthians 4:8-9; 2 Corinthians 4:16-18; 2 Corinthians 11:23-28*

## Scriptures on Anger

*Proverbs 14:17; Proverbs 14;29; Proverbs 10:12; Proverbs 12:16; Proverbs 17:9; Proverbs 19:11, 1 Peter 4:8; 1 Corinthians 13:4-5; Proverbs 15:1; Proverbs 30:33; Galatians 5:22-25; Ephesians 4:26*

## Scriptures on Bitterness, Resentment, and Hate

*Ephesians 4:31; Galatians 5:15; Galatians 5:19; Hebrews 12:15; 1 John 2:9-11; 1 John 3:11-20; 1 John 3:15*

# PRAYERS OF DELIVERANCE
## Chapter Thirteen

<hr>

## Forgiving Others - Personal Action

*F*orgiving others often starts as a decision of surrender-an act of our will. This surrender invites God to begin working in our lives in a deeper level, allowing God to heal us. Just as with anyone else, we can ask God to enlighten us with the understanding that we need to fully forgive from our hearts. We simply need to make the choice to be open to forgiveness and reconciliation.

As I close this book, I want to cover you in prayer and believe that you will take a leap of faith to remove yourself from spiritual abuse and become the person God created you to be. I pray that you will take the truth of what you just read and apply it to your own personal life. If you can't talk to others, you can always talk to God. He's waiting on you anyway. Nothing escapes Him.

## Prayer That Will Deliver and Set You Free
### FOR THE LAY PERSON

*Father God, in the name of Jesus, I pray that you will open my heart and help me repent of the deeds I have done, the negative effects on others I have caused, the lies I have told, and the harm and pain I have suffered and inflicted upon myself as I ignored your warnings. Please forgive me for choosing the enemy's ways over yours. Wash me in the blood and cleanse me from unrighteousness. Thank you for taking away the guilt and the shame from my lives and letting me feel your love. Protect me from the hands of the enemy as I get back in my rightful place. In Jesus name we pray, AMEN.*

*Father, I have gone through a lot of hurt and pain, but I want to be brought back into your presence. I have abandoned your ways because of what others have done to me and blamed you for it. Please forgive me and help me to find the right church to fellowship and grow up spiritually in. Lead me in the right paths and remove every inch of bitterness, strife, and hate from my spirit. Precious Lord, it is with a changed attitude that I come boldly before your throne. I choose to forgive all those who have wronged me and I choose to forgive myself. Help me to put away everything that does not honor you and focus only on those things that will cause me to grow and develop into the king/queen you made me to be. Let me walk with a pure conscience and serve you with pure motives. Rebuild my trust and confidence in the body of Christ without reservations. I thank you that you waited for me to make the right choices and return to the fold. I love you so much and desire to serve you with all my heart. Thank you for always being there and for forgiving me. You're the best Father any child could have. In Jesus name I pray, AMEN!*

*LORD, you know my heart and all the things that have kept me out of your presence. I have let what others did have an effect on our relationship and severed my own ties with you. I have believed what the enemy has said and went further into sin that I wanted to. Today I need the courage and ability to face my own truth and receive forgiveness for blind sight and blaming others for what I should have spoken up about. Thank you for releasing m from the guilt I've carried for so long and allowing me to feel the power of your love, the warmth of your embrace, and the fragrance of your presence back into my life. Help me to never stray from you again. Teach me your Word so I will follow the truth. With thanksgiving and praise, I lift your name on high. Thank you for your grace and mercy. In your son, Jesus name. Amen.*

God already knows the situation before you come before him. Be honest and sincere and watch God change things in your life. He never leaves us even when we're the messed-up ones. As leaders, we have to be honest and committed to teach the Word of God in totality, not bits and pieces or out of context.

## Prayer for the Repentant Leader

*Father God, as a leader that have led people astray from you, a s a leader that has put my own agenda before yours, as a servant that has abused your people for worldly gain. I humble myself before you today, asking for forgiveness and restoration. I have hurt and battered many of your sheep as I used your word to get what I needed through the church. It was not my intention to cause so much hurt and pain, but I admit that I did and want to be free from the guilt and shame it brings. Help me to hold my head up high and walk in the love you have provided for me. Help me to be truthful and repentant toward my congregation and show them a different me from this day forward. I receive your forgiveness and thank you for allowing me to get it right now, before death came to me. I love you for who you are and for who you will cause me to become. Let my fleshly nature die so that your spiritual nature will have full reign in me. I give you glory, honor, and praise. In Jesus name I pray. Amen.*

FATHER, I have been ensnared by some of Satan's attractions which I now know that they were put there to destroy me, but I know Jesus came to destroy the works of Satan. I desire to be free from every enticement and trap that he has set for me. Wash my mind, cleanse my heart, renew my strength in you to boldly come to the throne of grace and receive your mercy and forgiveness. I sell out to you this day and ask you to cleanse my conscience from dead works so I can serve the living God in spirit and in truth. I denounce every work of darkness I have been involved in and rejoice in your word which frees me from sin. Nothing will separate me from your love. Thank you for never leaving me or giving up on me. I n Jesus name. Amen.

Prayers do not have to be long, just pure, and sincere, showing a repentant attitude toward the offense committed and a genuine change of mind resulting in a different course of action.

Just in case you have not received Jesus as your personal Savior, pray this prayer that you may become part of the body of Christ

## Prayer for the Sinner

*Heavenly Father, I submit my will to you will. I know that you have plans for my life to give me a good future. I believe that Jesus is your son and that he died for me, was buried, resurrected and the n ascended to heaven to restore my relationship back with you. I renounce every evil work, every sin that I have committed and I accept JESUS as my SAVIOR and LORD. I submit my will to yours and accept your plans and purposes for my life. Empower me with the Holy Spirit to complete the work you have for me. Help me to make wise decisions in line with your word so that others will be blessed and drawn into the family of God. I believe with my heart and confess you as Lord with my mouth, therefore I am saved. Thank you for saving me. In Jesus name. AMEN.*

# ABOUT THE AUTHOR

Dr. Angela R. Williams – 1959, of Orangeburg, South Carolina is the second oldest of seven children. She graduated from Orangeburg-Wilkinson High School in 1977and furthered her education at Orangeburg-Technical College and Voorhees College. Dr. Williams graduated cum laude from Benedict College in 1995 with a bachelor of science degree in business administration.

In 1997, she graduated from Columbia International University with a master of arts degree in elementary education.

She has also received her Ed. S. degree in educational leadership from Cambridge College, also a bachelor of Biblical Studies from the International School of Religion, a masters and doctor of divinity from the Spirit of Truth Institute in Richmond, Virginia, and doctor of Philosophy and Christian education degree from the Institute of Christian Works in Seattle, Washington. Dr. Williams is a licensed and ordained Minister of the gospel and has been preaching since August, 1986.

Dr. Williams is Founder and Pastor of the explosive and growing Rejoice Christian Center, Inc. in Columbia, South Carolina. She is following the purpose of God for her life and expects to see the church move forward as many souls are saved, healed, and set free from all types of spiritual abuses.

Dr. Williams' authored her freshman book, **FREE NOT LOCKED UP ANYMORE**, May, 2015; which is a collection of poetry.

# RESOURCES

*Spiritual Abuse Network (S.A.N.) – where people can find grace to recover and move forward*

**Suggested Books to read:**
*Leadership that Builds People by Jim Richards*
*Soul Repair by Jeff VanVonderen*
*Healing Spiritual Abuse by Ken Blue*
*You are God's Best by T.L Osborn*

**Websites:**
*www.dtl.org/cults*
*www.nacronline.com/videos-workshops*
*www.relevantmagazine.com/god/church/its-time-address-spiritual-abuse-church*
*www.spiritualabuse.com*

**Bibliography**
**Daugherty**, Sharon. *Avoiding Deception (Victory Christian Center, 1997*
**Lambert**, Steven. *Charismatic Captivation, Authoritarian Abuse and Psychological Enslavement in Neo-Pentecostal Churches (Real Truth Publications, 1996)*
**Moore**, Beth. *Praying God's Word (B & H Publishing Group, 2009*
**Osteen**, John. *Deception, Recognizing True and False Ministries, (Osteen Publications, 1986)*
**Riley**, Carleen. *Help, I Want to Stop Hurting, A Guide to Forgiveness (Buckhead and Easton Publishing, 2010*
**Smith**, Louise. *Beyond the Clouds (Kingdom Builders Publication, 2014*

CPSIA information can be obtained at www.ICGtesting.com
Printed in the USA
BVIW12n0454191017
497836BV00012B/68